ROAD POEMS
U.S.A.

Poetry And Photographs From The Highways And Byways Of America

Cat Cohen

OTHER BOOKS by CAT COHEN

Road Horizon Division

CAT TRACKS – A Budget Train Travel Adventure (2018)
A frugal, insightful, and flavorful journey across the U.S. by train and rent-a-car from the colorful desert southwest to the historic coastal northeast.

MY DESERT BLOG CABIN (2009/2013)
A real estate memoir of how the author came to build his home in a rural settlement twenty miles north of Palm Springs.

TALES OF A CENSUS WORKER (2011)
A journal of the author's experiences while canvassing small town citizens, horse ranchers, fearful Hispanics, and anti-government holdouts for the 2010 census in the Southern California high desert.

ROAD STORIES SOUTHWEST (2010/2013)
Way-Off-the-beaten-path travel adventures from three journeys in New Mexico, Arizona, Southern Colorado and Northeastern Baja California.

THE LONGER ROAD HOME (2015)
An inspiring novel of recovery narrated by Sam Freberg, a bohemian Jewish musician born into a dysfunctional LA family in the 1940s. He describes his struggle for self-acceptance as a gay man, and how he combats addictions and an AIDS diagnosis.

Savory Publications Division

CHICKEN SOUPS FROM AROUND THE WORLD (2011)
Chicken soup recipes from 39 countries covering techniques and ingredients from equatorial Africa to arctic Alaska and very many temperate zones.

WHINE CONNOISSEUR'S GUIDE (2009/2013)
co-author Avry Budka   A tongue-in-cheek guide to the history of whines, whinemaker's art, whining and dining, whines for every occasion.

DIVING OUT IN LA (1984/1986)
co-author Avry Budka   A nostalgic and witty cult classic guide to the best low-cost eateries in the Greater Los Angeles area during the 1980s.

Koan Music Division

WRITING AND MARKETING SONGS FOR AN ORIGINAL ACT (2013)
An informative discussion of important songwriting issues questions such as performance, message, audience, genre, style, and industry format.

ROAD POEMS U.S.A.

Written by Cat Cohen
Photographs by Cat Cohen
Cover photo courtesy of Create Space

C 2010/2018 [David] Cat Cohen

ISBN # 978-0-9899390-6-5

Library of Congress Control Number 2018904814
Published by Cat Cohen Unltd

Printed in the United States of America

CAT COHEN UNLTD

PO Box 275
Morongo Valley, CA 92256

cat@catcohen.com
www.catcohen.com
www.catcohenauthor.com

1st Edition – May, 2010
2nd Edition – April, 2018

INTRODUCTION

Road Poems U.S.A. is a collection of observations and personal experiences from my many travels across this bountiful nation of ours from 1985 to 2007. Some of my journeying was with partners and/or friends, but most of this was solo travel. On my own, I was able to follow my natural curiosity wherever it led, opening me to less trodden paths. Without having someone nearby to share my experiences with, I was motivated to write my adventures down. Pen and paper can be a comfort in one's solitude. Some of these poems were written on paper napkins in coffee shops, while others notated in notebooks I took along on my trips. Additional ones were composed later on when I reflected on my experiences in front of my computer.

I've included photographs to add a visual dimension to these descriptions where they are available and appropriate. During this 20-year span, camera technology changed greatly. My early shots were taken with single reflex equipment. Many of the mid-period photos were made with portable disposables, and the more recent shots done with digital cameras.

Having been a music teacher and songwriter most of my life, composition comes easily to me. Combining poetry and photography is another way for me to express my creativity. I enjoy focusing on the uniqueness of each city, state, and region I visit, hoping in my small way to preserve some of the unique local color, texture, sensuality and personality that is being threatened by the sameness of corporate America.

Cat Cohen

ACKNOWLEDGMENTS

I want to pay tribute to some American poets who extolled the virtues and exposed the vices along our nation's roads way before me. First and foremost is Walt Whitman, who celebrated the American experiences of his time with passion and unbridled honesty. Robert Frost is another poet who comes to mind with his roads traveled and not traveled. Novelists who also shaped my writing include Mark Twain, John Steinbeck, and Jack Kerouac. Another source of inspiration has been Japanese haiku. Although I write outside its formal seventeen-syllable structure, I try to incorporate this art form's terse conciliation of differing perceptions of sensual images, especially when describing natural phenomena.

On a more personal level, I also want to acknowledge my friend and fellow creative writer, the late Vytautas Pliura, a poet known for his provocative, sometimes radical verse, yet he also expressed his softer side with sentimental water colors recalling much of his childhood growing up in the Midwest. A supportive artistic soul, he was a source of encouragement.

Lastly, I want to thank several people in my creative circle who have lent me their ears and given me feedback on my efforts. These include my editor Avry Budka, videographer Jennifer Ingle, composer Michael Viens, and my good friend Stina Jacobson.

TABLE OF CONTENTS

Afoot and light-hearted, I take to the open road,
          healthy, free, the world before me,
The long brown path before me,
          heading wherever I choose.

Henceforth I ask not good-fortune,
          I myself am good fortune;
Henceforth I whimper no more, postpone no more
          need nothing, strong and content
          I travel the open road.

Walt Whitman

SOUTHWEST

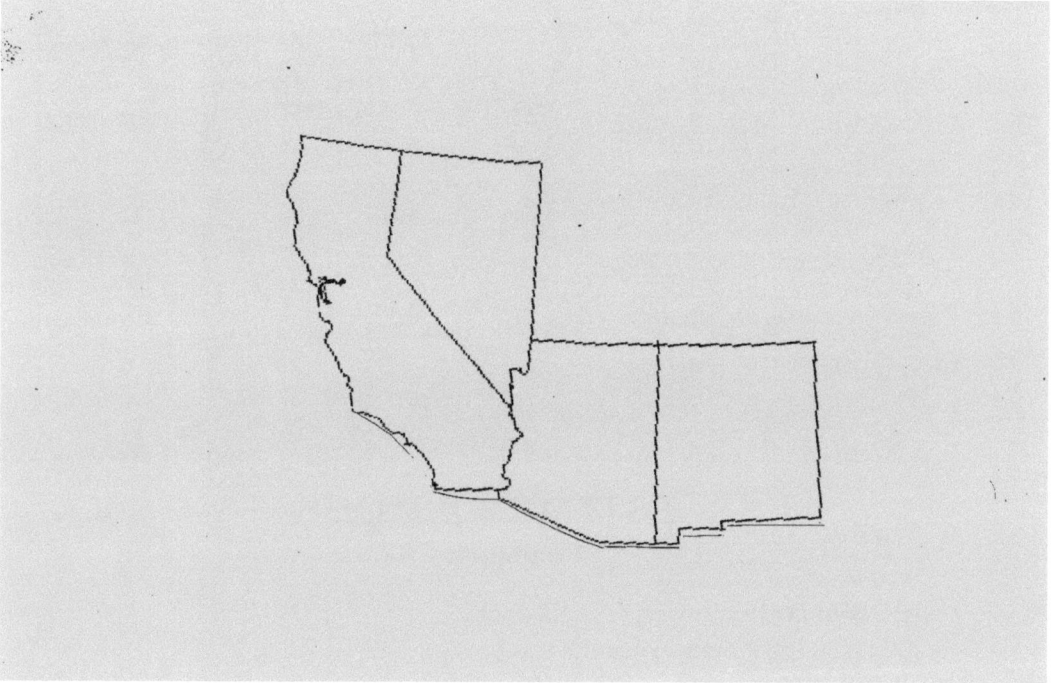

The Southwest has a unique history with its strong Native American and Hispanic heritage, gold fever mentality, and stark contrasts between the sparse, arid, wild-west settlements and the high-paced glitzy entertainment industry centers like Hollywood and Las Vegas. From trendsetting California to the widely scattered desert communities in Arizona and New Mexico, there is a sense of personal freedom of expression and informality bordering on the unconventional.

CALIFORNIA

ESTUARY BRIDGE
(Alameda, CA)

Pleasure boats float lazily moored in their docks
    as autos slowly cross the steel gray estuary bridge
Though a handsome distance from the salty water below
    this proud connector rises even higher when tall ships call
On this tranquil Sunday only small craft prevail
    so no one needs to wait for this bridge to rise or fall

ANOTHER COLD SIERRA MORNING
(Florence Lake, CA)

While trout fishermen cast flies across her crest
    angling for German browns and rainbows
    to ingest the allure of shiny metal
    snowdrifts pile up on the steel gray cemented holders
    of frigid water in her reservoir
Rivulets seep into her bosomy bed
    multiplying into the massive body she now stores
    as craggy pines rise above her rocky shores
    outboard motors hiss and roar breaking the timeless silence
Florence Dam collects herself
    for another cold Sierra morning

WHIRLWIND
(Anza Borrego, CA)

While banks of fog cling to the sandy floor of this arid open air home
        Anza Borrego attempts some house cleaning
        with a little tempest to sweep things in order
Dust and sand gather about in a whirlwind
        circular motion rearranges some leaves in the dry brush
        a winding trail of broken twigs says that this room is done

THE COVE'S LOWER BEDROOM
(La Jolla, CA)

Sliding, slippery, sloshing, splashing tidepool waves
        spin circular paths over smooth eroded rocks
Once the tide is out in the cove's lower bedroom
        anenome and starfish sun themselves on the watery deck
As sea grass forms an impromptu lawn
        graciously extending itself into the Pacific

ALICE'S CAFE
(Bakersfield, CA)

Early AM sees this eatery fill with men with hats
        from construction to sombrero, oil rigger to caballero
        Alice waits on 'em all, calling them by their first names
Serving up home cooking to today's Pancho Villas
        her motto through the years has been
        boost a man's ego and fill his need to be one of her boys
        local machos know full well the way she treats her clientele
Most of her business is repeat
        for a gal pushing fifty, quite a nifty feat

THREE ORANGES
(Terra Bella, CA)

Braking for the Oranges For Sale sign, I turned into the grove
        as a tall lanky youth greeted me slowly while I drove
When I asked him what oranges were selling for
        he replied "no comprendo senor"
So in broken Spanish I repeated my request
        and with not much more zest he replied
        "No ees open, lo siento mucho" he said politely
        while my sense of sorry was much more mighty
As I started to leave, making sure he wasn't watching
        I grabbed from a tree a treasured fruit
        when I heard him following in hot pursuit
Turning around, I expected a stern reprimand
        but instead he had cradled in his large brown hands
        perfectly large round as could ever be
        three sweet juicy oranges he had picked just for me

IRRIGATION STILL LIFE
(Buttonwillow, CA)

Irrigated water flows where crops grow on the banks of Interstate 5
        trucks great and small stopping along this field for a breather
        with engine still humming and driver out on a fast food forage
Big wheels rest with cargoed storage
        the gurgle of piped water is heard as well as seen
        soothing the travail of both man and machine

OBSERVATORY LANDSCAPE
(Los Angeles, CA)

Many points of light flicker as sunrays bend fading paths over LA
        purplish-pink, the sky turns pastel
        while streetlights and silhouettes take on nocturnal colors
Surveying this urban landscape from an observatory view
        a pair of lovers clasp hands as one vista is felt by two

HITCHHIKER
(Goleta, CA)

I met myself on Highway 101
> half my age with backpack and extended thumb the world exploring
> with wide blue eyes, long blond hair and a smile imploring
> exchanging a friendly vibe for a ride north

Feeling like company I opened my car door to this stranger who was no stranger
Eighteen years previously I had stood thumb outstretched on the very same offramp
> I decided to repay a debt from the carefree trails I'd once made

This lanky youth climbed in throwing his pack onto the back seat
> sporting a bandana that held his curly strands in check

Telling of his trek from Oregon to Texas flagging rides from truckers,
> hopping freight trains at small town tracks until he got caught

Now he was standing north of Santa Barbara
> with an Oregon homecoming on his mind

His lack of paranoia even after a few highway misadventures
> a testament to the idealism of his tender years

His small town perspective put mine in retrospective
> remembering when doors were left unlocked
> and strangers welcomed with open arms without any harm

He talked of growing up with lumberjacks in logging towns
> with hard winter snow on the ground
> of being on his own since the age of sixteen,

Seeing life as a game of chess, choosing his moves slowly, but not afraid to take risks
He talked about his love of symbols and words, his favorite image a high-flying bird
> revealing fights he'd been forced into

One night stands he'd made love to and tears he'd cried over both
> more sensitive than one might expect from a vagabond his age

Many miles and a few hours later I gave him some cash for the road
> leaving him and his load at a truck stop in Gilroy half man, half boy,
> ready to make another move on his chessboard north

Part of me still travels with him
> chasing adventure where the fog intersects the sun
> freeing myself on Highway 101

DATE PLANTATION
(Indio, CA)

One palm seems to blend into the next as rows of fronds fall into
> formation like a military band doing maneuvers

The harsh sun heats well over one hundred degrees
> except in the cooler clearings under these cross-hatched trees
> where tiny brown globes hang like earrings from the branches

their sweet dry fruit dotting these desert ranches
Down the road they'll teach you about the sex life of these dates
then pick some and make a shake out of their mates

HOUSE OF SOLITUDE
(Mission Soledad, CA)

In this house of solitude
Our Lady reigns in an empty room alone with her meditations
Votive candles burn as she waits for a response to her incantations
with the Father, Son and Holy Ghost monitoring upstairs
she needs to know someone on earth really cares
Today not a soul is around to hear her prayers
only the thick adobe walls have ears

THIRSTY RAINDANCE
(Pearblossom, CA)

Tall, slender, spiny with clumps
of dusty green patches hanging from their trunks

Joshuas spring from their bunks on the desert floor
              after a sudden downpour answers their thirsty prayer
Stretching their appendages in a grateful dance
              having patiently done without through months of drought
              these sand dwellers drink every last drop into their barreled chests

FOG DAYS OF MIDSUMMER
(Muir Beach, CA)

I walked the beach in the gloom of a cold gray afternoon
              dense clouds wrapped around me filling
              this August day with weather so chilling it felt like December
My lips turned blue and face turned whiter
              the lemonade I brought should have been hot cider
              my light clothing forced me to seek the heat at a group's bonfire
The shore was filled with barbecuers grilling skewers
              kids playing with beach-balls running in circles on the moist sand
Their canines, half Eskimo and half otter, diving into the frigid water
              chasing balls being thrown as I was getting frozen to the bone
Nippier than a winter holiday, I left the hardy souls in play before I became number
              in the dog days, the fog days of midsummer

WAKING TO A SUNLIGHTED PINE
(Mount Pinos, CA)

A loud blood-curdling shriek from a high flying bird at daybreak
        awoke me from the deep as cold mountain air made its creep
        into the mouth of my sleeping bag
I flapped my arms in protest to no avail
        as sunlight's first rays poured onto the mountain trail
While cursing the cold I gazed from earth to sky
        and found a golden sight for sore eyes
        yellow light streaming through a pine tree above
The warming soil around my forest bed cooled my temper as well
        I soon forgave my noisy feathered friend his raucous yell

OLD ITALIAN DINNERS
(Porterville, CA)

One dark gray day I saw a cafe with peeling plaster, rusted screens, roof in decay
        and a large ITALIAN DINNERS sign in antique neon
        shocked to find that it was still open, I ventured inside to see
        two middle-aged waitresses and customers three

When I inquired about the its history
        the women recalled when loggers and miners were in demand
        hired hands speaking native tongues in this center for food and fun

On occasion more than dining went on in this rustic location
        inside the rear bungalows quaint and crude
        the workmen met up with prostitutes raising hell during good times
        'til the logging got thin and the boss closed the mine

Long since its heyday saucy tales are kept alive thanks to these spinners
        serving up the past as another tasty dish to go
        to satisfy the curiosity of those like me who wish to know
        the truth behind these old Italian dinners

OAK, BARN AND TRAILER
(Oroville, CA)

Oak, barn and trailer sit unattended in the hot Central Valley noon
        as farmer and workers take time out from the morning's chores
        with sounds of siesta snores emanating from the back
        things not shaded boil, bake and fry under the relentless sun
Despite the dry heat, soon all will be back on their feet
        cultivating another day of progress toward harvest

OVERCAST
(Ventura, CA)

Alone with the elements
        the surf fisherman blends in with the overcast
        his line tossed and turned by the waves
The elusive prize he seeks to beach has stayed well out of reach
        but there's still hope he'll find his match in a silver lined catch

NEVADA

WATERING HOLES
(Indian Springs, NV)

With saloons on each side of Highway 95
   this pit stop is a break from the desert desolation
   where coffee and conversation
   blends with Nevada cowboys wearing boots and western duds

After downing endless schooners of suds they go outside to smoke what the heck
   and scratch their gray beards and red necks

Not a drinker and not a smoker not the kind to play video poker
If I lived in these parts I'd likely join the crew and their vices too

CASINO FEVER
(Las Vegas, NV)

What lurks at the end of the glitzy rainbow where light bulbs blink, streak and glow
   fanning rich expectations of gamblers from 50 states with neon bait
   from early mornings to wee hours late

Rows of one-armed bandits soak the sundry nickel, quarter and silver dollar hungry
   with cherry, orange and plum splashing fountains of jangling silver
   even though most of the profits will be pilfered
   except for a fortunate few who escape with a jackpot or two

Card games surround gaming tables on velveted lawns of greens
   for those of various means from lowlife to high roller scenes
   from curious and spurious to desperate and furious
   eager to take a shot at the proverbial pot of gold
   when the bright lights of casino fever takes hold

TEST SITE
(Mercury, NV)

Off-road, off limits, high security clearance needed
   to visit or otherwise explore
When tough warning signs heeded
   my curiosity abated
   and the urge to wander
   changed direction to a different wild blue yonder

ARIZONA

SKELETON OF A HOUSE
(Bisbee, AZ)

A skeleton of a house sits atop a hill
       in a forgotten ghost town neighborhood
       a few bends around a winding canyon away
       from the beds and breakfasts of Bisbee reborn
Residents and tourists line up in the high desert morn
       while this forlorn frame pines away for even a single visitor

ICE CREAM, COLD POP, SMALL TALK
(Duncan, AZ)

Franklin store sits squarely on the foundation of its small town success
Neighborly in a neighborhood where neighbors are few
        holding onto its loyal clientele with an art it knows so well
No double coupons or lottery games can compare to the grocer who really cares
        about what's news in his customers' lives

LONG DISTANCE TRUCKERS
(Buckeye, AZ)

A long distance trucker and his lady park at a local coffee shop as it gets dark
        savoring a home cooked meal on the run
        before hauling freight down the Interstate
        whatever the big farmers need to go Eastward ho
Lemons to St. Louis, cotton to Chattanooga,
        lettuce to Charlotte, pitted dates to Atlanta
Then returning to the old homestead, a well-heated room and a welcome soft bed
        'til it's get the rig ready for that lonely stretch of highway once again

NAVAJO PINES
(Lukachukai Mountains, AZ)

High atop a sacred hill
        dark green needles and honey brown cones
        hover over rolling mounds of red earth tones
        as mysterious breezes blow through evergreen branches
        downslope to Indian summer ranches
Remnants of snow pack thaw and bake in the ancestral sun
        as spirits of sky, water, earth, and trees all become one

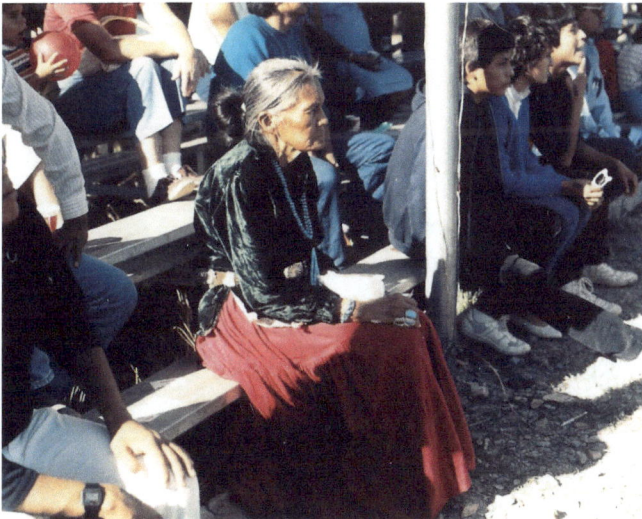

LOYALTY TO THE TRIBE
(Fort Defiance, AZ)

Sitting in the bleachers wearing her tribal best
> cheering on the dancers in animal feathered vests

Her memory flashes back to a young brave
> she once helped prepare for this ceremony
> in her younger days when they talked of matrimony

Alcohol aborted his sacred vows
> taking him from his warrior bows in his prime
> before they could join their hearts for all time

Now as new celebrators pass by her view
> she commemorates the tried and true
> and demonstrates her loyalty to the tribe anew

TRADING POST
(Ganado, AZ)

Old dark brown rocks mortared into stone walls
> rusted wagon wheels outside beckon shoppers into its halls

Navajo merchandise are stacked up in rows on sale
> rugs, blankets, kachinas, jewelery prevail
> goods enough to fill a department store with authentic crafts and lore

If I had a bulging wallet I know it would soon be toast at this bountiful trading post

GEMBOREE
(Quartzsite, AZ)

The gemboree in Quartzsite unfurls its booths to rockhounds who stop to pursue
> semi-precious metals and quasi-precious stones beads and rugs

Sand paintings and basketed tokens, truckers' caps with corny slogans
> dime store jewelery, off color T-shirts, and tourist tomfoolery

From snowbirds their homes forsaking
> To live in a swap meet of their own making

PAT'S SLEEPING BEAUTY BAR
(Globe, AZ)

Who knows what sleeping beauties patronize Pat's place
        searching for princes in this outpost saloon
        with charms enough to see through the make up on their face
        and turn their pumpkin lives into coaches
Early evening royalty seekers can afford to be choosy
        but as the night wears on beehived in booze-impaired visions
Princesses abandon the quest for dreamboats on the dance floor and settle for frogs
        the blue-collar workers willing to walk them out the front door

NO LAST CHANCE GAS STATION
(Peach Springs, AZ)

This last chance gas station's closing was sadly overdue
        A place where passing cars once got fixed
        before this memorial to the old Highway 66
        was 86'd by Interstate 40
Ethyl and her lower test relations
        no longer pump into the few cars crossing the reservation
        out of customers, out of cash, out of luck, and out of gas

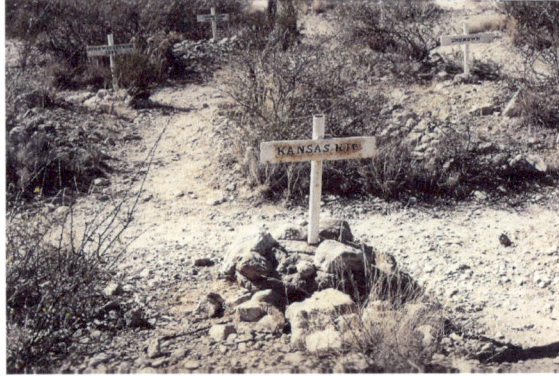

BOOT HILL
(Tombstone, AZ)

Remarkable and unremarkable pioneer families
        in marked and unmarked graves
        honored not for their honor or heroism
        remembered not for their great works or fortunes amassed
Some like the Kansas Kid and China Mary
        not even recalled by their real names
        but all memorialized just for being and dying here
        in their pride, shame and glory
        sons and daughters of the real Arizona territory

STILL LIFE IN YELLOW AND GRAY
(Union Pass, AZ)

Warm yellow sunrays slide through silvered openings in the cold gray cloud cover
        falling gently on already yellow strands of dried winter grass
        carpeting the rough rocky Northern Arizona plain
Majestic snow-lined gray peaks rise in the distance
        a counterpoint to the bright fusion of one yellow upon another
        as the blinding glare sets fire to the cool stillness of the afternoon
        rustic barbed-wire fences run their patchwork interference

NEW MEXICO

LUMENARIAS
(Albuquerque, NM)

Brown paper sacks filled with sand and candles
        form stacks in rows on decks of adobed stuccoes
        on shop railings and store windows
In Old Town this Christmas day the afternoon holds
        but a trail of last night's flickerings from these joyful lamps
Yet the smoke from candles extinguished
        lingers in the frosty air
These carolers of light wear their paper costumes intact
        ready for a repeat performance in the Albuquerque night

CHRISTMAS MORNING FREEZE
(Gallup, NM)

Christmas morning and all through Gallup not a creature is stirring
        except the spirits melting in last week's snow
Children of the Navajo will soon be waking
        to dive into package wrapped merry making
        shrieking in a universal language
        all young ones understand
Meanwhile in the thirty degree freeze
        deserted streets swept by the chilling breeze from the north
        sends shivers up any walker bold enough to venture forth

OLD PUEBLO
(Laguna, NM)

Rough hewn sand and stone
        sculptured brown forms in warm earth tones
        thick clay bricks layered into homes
This lone community somehow keeps its immunity
        from the rudely bustling Interstate in its front yard
In the old pueblo, a primitive condo where tech is low
        corn and squash trade for residence dues
        as well as handicrafts crying red and turquoise blues
Civilization hurriedly may skirt along its length
        while at this off-ramp time itself slowly harvests its strength

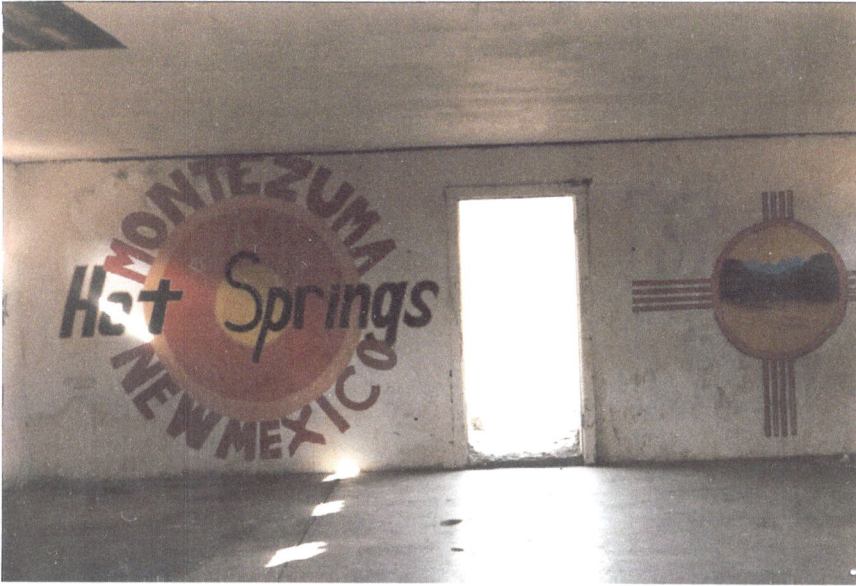

HOT AND COLD SPRINGS
(Montezuma, NM)

Abandon all warmth ye who enter here
       that is until you get into the heated water
       at this open-aired cement house of hydrotherapy
In wintry sub-freezing weather
       it's not as healing as it's reputed to be
One must be insane to endure the shock and pain
       of traveling from arctic to tropic temperatures and back again

CHILI STRINGS
(Santa Fe, NM)

Dark red thick veins, long pods tied in strings smelling fresca as salsa to be
    a piquant decorator's delight hanging from aging trucks
For a few bucks a New Mexicano will trade sun-dried anchos home made
    to tourists, artists and gourmets who know best
    the real color and flavor of the Southwest
In L.A. they hawk maps to the homes of the stars
    while this Santa Fe display entices cars with something much spicier

FRY BREAD TACO
(Shiprock, NM)

At a local swap meet where the natives shop and greet
    a woman at an improvised taco stand
    tosses corn batter into a hot oiled pan
Grilling pieces of sizzling lamb to fit on top of a bed
    of lettuce and tomato inside some freshly fried bread
With savory smells and bubbling sounds attracting passersby
    there was no way I could deny myself a taste
    of what Navajos like to munch
I could hardly wait to eat this savory treat
    pass the bottle of hot sauce
    I'm ready for lunch

NORTHWEST

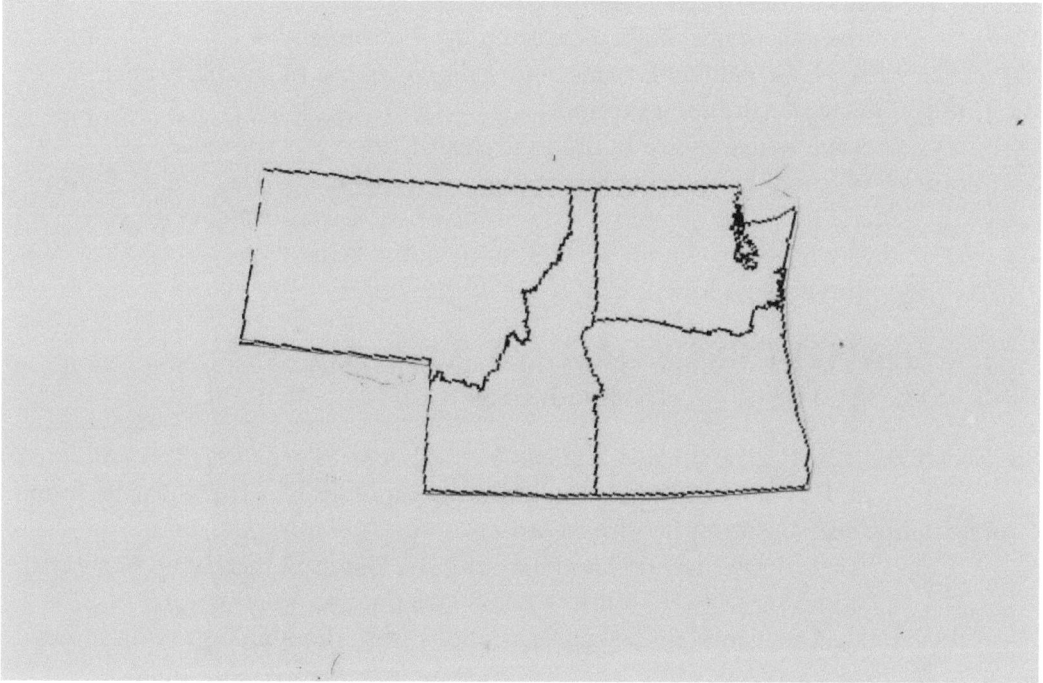

The Northwest mixes progressive and reactionary styles with a fine balance. In both the liberal urban centers of Seattle and Portland and the more conservative small towns from rural Oregon and Washington to Montana, a sense of libertarianism permeates all. Some of our nation's most beautiful verdant landscapes are set in open sky country with its vast horizons, while the cities reflect a contemporary pioneering spirit with a sophisticated sense of purpose and vision.

OREGON

TWO CITIES ADJACENT
(Medford/Ashland, OR)

There is hardly more contrast in style between two cities separated by very few miles
One, where rednecks defend their rights,
          the other with Shakespearean plays for the erudite
Cars in one village blast talk radio while actors nearby quote Juliet and Romeo
Gun toting collectors stand their ground
          while staged duels fight in the nearby town
Tract homes with monochrome colors and lines contrast mansions' unique designs
Parks with generic lawns and jungle gyms a stone's throw from statuary gardens
Like two siblings who've grown up differently from the start
          these two adjacent locales are worlds apart

BAND INSTRUMENT STREET SCENE
(Klamath Falls, OR)

The weekly roping off its main street allows local citizens to walk by, meet, and greet
          in this neighborly town where contemporary life style is hardly found
No top 40 musicians perform for the crowd
          instead tuba and trumpet players blare out loud marching music for
          admiring faces who throw coins into their waiting instrument cases
Down the block a Dixieland band swings as echoes from the buildings joyfully ring
          local citizens stroll by stores to sounds we hardly hear anymore

OLD FOLKS HOTEL
(Portland, OR)

In this downtown district people seldom observe
    a residential hotel that stills serves
    its elderly residents in a brick building so antique
    long past its prime while they are long past their peak

The octogenarians sit in their parlor staring into space
    on tattered once luxurious furniture seeming so out of place
    passing their sunset years of second childhood in reverse
    with assistance from counselor, doctor and nurse

Comparing the residence with its residents
    it's hard to say which came first

WASHINGTON

WHALING CANOE
(Neah Bay, WA)

The weather beaten canoe sits on its perch like a railcar on its trestle
> a testament to the days when it was a working vessel
> for groups of Makah to venture from the shore in boats
Searching for whales that swam along the coast
> throwing harpoons to harvest food
> to feed their families and heat their rooms
> with oil for lamps and soap for baths
Balancing the tribe's needs
> with respect of the creatures that once roamed so free

LOG PILES
(Vancouver, WA)

Logs are sorted and piled like pick up sticks
> by the wharf of the Columbia ready to be shipped
> far from where they were harvested

PUBLIC MARKET
(Seattle, WA)

An antique lettered neon sign calls tourists and locals to three-storied rows of stalls
        With fish, fowl, and produce displays of ingredients in vast arrays
Beckoning eager shoppers stop at cafes to snack after bargains at their favorite racks
        packaging fresh groceries in paper sacks
        gratefully filling their waiting arms for trips back home
        journeys with rewards more than food alone

BUZZ
(Seattle, WA)

Caffeine did not discover, settle, design or mentor
        this northwest urban center but almost defines it now
People buzz by on their way to and fro in search of the best coffee ground to go
        carrying the proverbial Starbucksian cup running over
Seagulls buzz in from the sound
        dotcomers buzz the trendy bars
        homeless buzz trying to sleep under the stars
        museums buzz the latest artists
        tourists buzz the public market
At every corner espresso is the common denominator
        latte a mood determinator
        with so much java who needs food
Slow motion is for smaller venues
        when java headlines all the menus
        in Seattle the pace is fast because...... of all the buzz

MONTANA

SHOOTING A MOUNTAIN GOAT
(Glacier National Park, MT)

A herd of snow-white big-horned beasts
   topped the rocky crags to the east of the main road
   as these wild goats grazed in their protected mountain home
   I gazed with fascination afraid to risk their alienation
If I so much was to snap my camera's shutter
   I'd send the whole lot of them a-flutter with its noise
   preventing me from capturing the visual joys I wanted to own
Attempting to get off a shot with skill and cunning
   I did indeed send them running
   but not before my lens stored for preservation
   a peek at an awesome creature in its glacial park location

WILD WOOLY WELCOME
(Hot Springs, MT)

In the tiny town of Hot Springs where visitors are few
   healing waters are piped into the lone hotel
A public park nearby has an outdoor pool
   filled from the very same well
I changed into my bathing suit and plunged right in
   to feel some mineral warmth upon my skin
Then a group of young locals crashed
   this tranquil place before I could relax
   jumping inside with rough loud voices

Telling tall tales of braggadocio choices
>> crimes committed and arrests made
>> court cases and prison escapades
>> that made me want to disappear for fear of my life
These seemingly juvenile delinquents made me so uneasy
>> I started planning an escape route merely to survive
When two sheriffs in uniform disrobed and joined the lively throng
>> even wilder tales were strung
>> of chasing deadbeats and fights with guns
>> confrontations while wearing bulletproof vests
>> all of this putting my courage to the test
Whether this was for their entertainment or mine
>> their out of town guest
>> I was given a wild wooly welcome to the mountain west

COWBOY BAR
(Hot Springs, MT)

Not much larger than a cabin's living room
>> with barely enough stools to call itself a saloon
>> this Montanan small business, while far from grand
>> quenches the thirsts of many a ranch hand
If there aren't any bullet holes in its dusty walls
>> there's been more than its share of barroom brawls
Yet compared to western movies the place is nowhere as rowdy
>> mostly folks stopping by to clink glasses
>> spin yarns and say howdy

MIDWEST

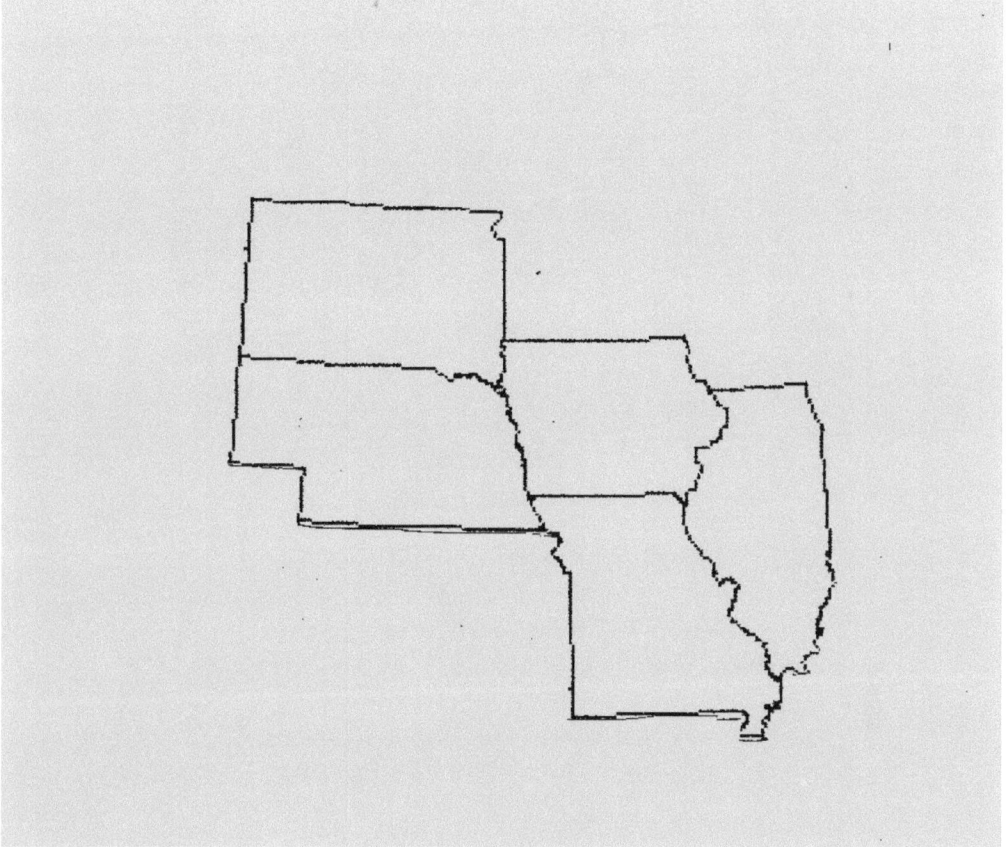

The Midwest region is rich in simple unaffected ways of living from its clean friendly cities to its abundant fertile farmland. Steeped in Native American history and flush with settlements bordering its wide rivers, this part of the U.S. tends to revere its traditions. From silos in South Dakota to Indian reservations in Nebraska to Confederate flags waving near the levees of Southern Missouri to city parks and folksy county fairs in Illinois, there is much to witness and commemorate.

SOUTH DAKOTA

SHINY SILO HOME
{Parker, SD)

Tall round canisters of steel rise up to their scaffolds
        where grainy storage is put on hold
        for cattle forage or a rainy day in this northern plains town
        surrounded by soil fertile dark brown
Hidden from view like gold nuggets in a mine
        these riches wait for their appointed time
        reaped and stored long after they've been sown
        to feed the hungry in their shiny silo home

OUT OF THE SAME RED ROCKS
(Sioux Falls, SD)

Just a few blocks away
        downtown buildings are built out of the same rocks
        as the floor of what this city calls its namesake falls
Strong enough to withstand a climate extreme
        whether it be rushing water from the burgeoning stream
        flowing over the top or blizzards falling in mid-winter non-stop
The stalwart settlers built their structures to stand on their own
        these massive edifices hewn out of red granite and stone

NOT SO MIDDLE-AMERICAN MUSIC MUSEUM
(Vermillion, SD)

In a part of our nation where music is more like a hoedown
        a startling collection of exotic instruments can be found
        an unlikely site for harpsichords, lutes and antique guitars
        marimbas, gamelan gongs, vinas and sitars
Gathered from eras of history and far away grounds
        displayed for students of ethnic sounds
It's a pleasure to listen to as well as to see 'em
        at this not so Middle-American music museum

SPIRIT MOUND
(Vermillion, SD)

Not far from where the wide Missouri leaves its mark
        an earthen hill once visited by Lewis and Clark
        overlooks prairie wildflowers and grasses
Buffalo once roamed in teeming masses
        and Native Americans worshipped the land and its wealth
Maybe the spirits who tend this preserve in repose
        will look after the evening primrose
        as butterflies flutter by asters and milkweeds
        sipping nectar and spreading seeds
        replenishing what this area needs

NEBRASKA

FOUR WINDS AND A CROSS
(Blair, NE)

At a site beside a Lutheran college's hallowed ground
> a shrine to the merging of two religions can be found
> a rainbow colored cross cries out with Christian care
> to share beliefs with a common prayer

Reaching out to the four winds and four directions
> of the original native Americans
> chants for the ancestor spirits' protection
A mosaic of Black Elk's vision before he was injured cruelly
> at the massacre at Wounded Knee

He recovered and later married
> two different Christian woman before he was buried
> having joined new practice and old tradition
> working to improve his people's condition

Now we pay homage to his rise from tragedy
> and give honor to his memory
> pooling supernatural forces
> merging advice from two higher sources

RESERVATIONS NOT REQUIRED
(Macy, NE)

In this small reservation town two men hang out
        in front of a tiny grocery store walking about
        while children play games in a nearby schoolyard
An old Christian church raises its steeple
        but the native religion is nowhere to be seen
        which doesn't mean it's not practiced here, just not openly

CHEAP ROADSIDE REST
(South Sioux City)

This small town late one summer night had few motels vacant, only this one in sight
        it was plain to see this accommodation was absent any luxury
Needing to rest my weary bones I paid at the office for this temporary home
With trepidation I went to the room and turned the key
        to sparse furniture and decoration and an old TV with few stations
The bulky mattress comforted this tired dog and all night I slept like a log

until a rooster crowed as dawn lit up the dark
   outside the window was a water tower and trailer park
I soaked in the venerable bathroom's antique tiled tub
   and in this nostalgic setting I shaved, soaped and scrubbed
Returning to my car I felt strangely refreshed
   for half the price I had twice the fun in this cheap roadside rest

RAILCARS ACROSS THE RIVER
(South Sioux City)

On a bridge that spans the muddy Missouri
   freight trains go across without any hurry
   to and fro between two cities named Sioux

Banging and clanging the way railcars do
   breaking the quiet with horns and bells
   they traverse the water with their mechanical yells

Car after car slithers over the tracks
   a hundred plus from front engine to back
   soon after the noise quits its mighty roar
   the caboose waves farewell and there's silence once more

IOWA

HUNTING IN THE FROG POND
(Desoto Wildlife Refuge)

In an oxbow where a winding river once broke loose
        is a large pond friendly to duck, eagle and goose
Wildlife teems in these bogs with lily pads and sunning frogs
        a protected haven of natural wonders
        safe from all but a few hunters in season
        signs warn all to limit their decoys within reason
        one's shooting powers only allowed from dawn to dusk hours
As tempting as this food chain is for hungry birds
        if they could read English they'd spread the word
        other bodies of water are better off for their flight
        smart ones would be wise to stay here only at night

HOME COOKING LOUNGE
(Council Bluffs)

Just across the river from Omaha's bustle
        an old Iowa suburb does the working man's hustle
They take it easy this side of the tracks
        even the sleazy bars want their customers to relax
One lounge doesn't brag that their ladies are good looking
        but the sign says they serve up home cooking
Does that mean when the regulars hang up their hats
        they're asked by the girls "do you want fries with that?"

THE GOLDEN SPOON
(Sioux City)

In this city named Sioux I chose to eschew
        the corporate chain eateries on the main drag
Searching the downtown district 'til I could find
        a folksy homey touch for a meal back in time
Behind gingham curtained windows
        was a greasy spoon without too much grease
        where the conversation warmed as it increased

All-American eggs and such
        and biscuits and jam with a homemade touch
        were prepared with pleasure to slowly savor
I sat at a table and read through a local paper
        as I enjoyed a meal with down home service, price and flavor

Every town could use one of these cafes to brighten up one's days
        if I lived nearby I'd be returning soon to the Golden Spoon

MISSOURI

CAJUN SAMPLING
(Cape Girardeau, MO)

Sedate mansions overlook the muddy Mississippi's shores
     above a row of old shops and stores
     while in the middle of the block a Cajun café
     serves up jumbalaya, red beans, rice, and estoufee

After sampling tasty gumbo and savory down home stew
     I wanted try the whole menu
     but would have needed a two-week stay
     to accomplish this quest

I told the proprietors their food was the best
     and wishing to revisit this sweet refrain
     I begged them in vain to open a branch out west

LONE LIBERALS ON THE LEVEE
(Cape Girardeau, MO)

Confederate flags fly here abundantly
       showing this region's slave state history
       and I from a place that's been known for liberation
       in a keep my opinions to myself situation

Walking down by the levee as the water moved south
      I resolved not to open my progressive mouth
      when I passed a couple wearing buttons that read
      I'm proud to be a liberal

I called out to them with a casual line
      it was a pleasure to speak no longer clandestine
      and conversation came easily with their views like mine
Then, so far to the left, they spoke of such utopian dreams
      that even I felt put off by their radical schemes
In their ideal catch phrases they seemed to be caught
      soon I no longer agreed with the beliefs they bought
When they had no interest in hearing my views
      I could hardly wait for our talk to be through
This sudden openness soon came to naught
      maybe I'm more of a redneck than I thought

LITTLE ITALY
(St. Louis, MO)

In a part of mid-city dolled up in old brick is a venerable neighborhood very ethnic
      residential at first glance but if one stops here by chance
      hidden in this camouflaged haunt most corners house an Italian restaurant

Many red, white and green flags of pride salute their heritage from homes on all sides
      in architecture with little pretension
      this district hardly gets a mention in travel books
      yet after dining at one of these eateries so fine
      I gestured my highest compliments to the cooks

ILLINOIS

MUSIC IN GRANT PARK
(Chicago, IL)

John Phillip Souza never sounded so good
   as in this large tree-lined park in a downtown neighborhood
   blaring from speakers hung up on lampposts
   spreading music from the skyscrapers to Lake Michigan's coast
Compositions American for residents and guests
   who visit this grand metropolis of the Midwest

Band instruments morphed into orchestral sounds
   as Gershwin's Rhapsody In Blue blasted the surrounds
   the populace sunning themselves on dark green park benches
   rich and poor mingling without any fences

Other cities shy away from these classical names
   but Chicago trumpets them unashamed
   in Grant Park daily for all to hear it
   to raise vibrations as well as spirit
No Top 40 played or pop music canned
   but a virtual fanfare for the common man

SNOW CONE STAND
(Clinton, IL)

In this tiny town by a big river, small joys of life are delivered by hand
        by a jolly aproned woman who tends the snow cone stand
Locals can savor over one hundred flavors
        as they take their time choosing lemony-lime, blueberry dream,
        cherry vanilla or coconut supreme
        syrups to mix or match, artificial or on the natch
The lady fills a large paper cup with more than enough ice
        to beat the summer's heat with this sweet sticky vice
        that gives the palette a quick burst of cold
        that may rot a tooth or two, but is sure to soothe the soul

APPLE FESTIVAL WEEKEND
(Murphrysboro, IL)

I should have taken the bypass around
        as traffic on this small town street slowed to a trickle
By the time I realized my sad mistake
        there was a parade and I was stuck in the middle
Crowds of people were milling around me
        an apple festival celebration soon surrounded me

as my car, like molasses, crawled past the main town square
    I heard sweet bluegrass music travel through the air
Colorful booths of corn shucked fun much like a county fair
    with cotton candy, games, balloons and prizes
    and vendors with novelties of all sizes
    carnival barking and absolutely not a parking spot in sight
Rather than pray for this river of vehicles to end
    I grabbed my camera to shoot what I could not attend
    this tribute to rural life here in the Midwest
    seeing Americana truly at its best

LIVING SOUTHERN IN A NORTHERN STATE
(Cairo, IL)

Just north of Dixie in Mason land
    where two great rivers join their outstretched hands
Is a tranquil transplanted Mississippi town
    with ramshackle buildings, schools and playgrounds
Old movie houses neglected and a civic center rejected
    except where barbecue places and Baptist churches grace
    the slow pace that these Afro-American folk call home
No one seems to mind that this city has been so forgotten by time
    the lack of modern convenience shows no unease
As the overgrown trees shed their large deep green leaves
    on the wide dusty streets in the sweet Magnolia breeze
No sign of the populace being displeased
    about their peculiar fate of living Southern in a Northern state

SOUTH

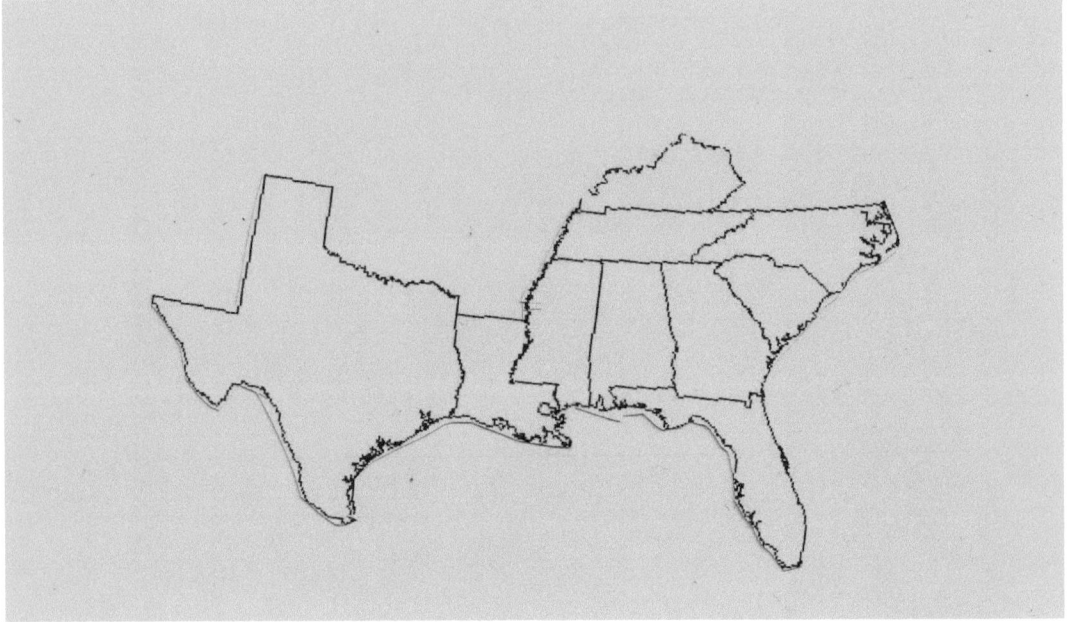

The South spans a large area filled with colorful history, vibrant cities, and lush greenery. From down home Kentucky and Tennessee to the sparse Texas plains to the swampy Louisiana bayous to fast paced Miami to the laid back Georgia and Carolina countryside, this part of America captivates and inspires one's imagination with its warm Southern hospitality laced with an underlying streak of decadence.

KENTUCKY

DIGGING DIRT AT A DIXIE LAUNDROMAT
(Paducah, KY)

There can be quite a window to a city's soul
        in a neighborhood laundromat on the road
        eavesdropping on the locals while washing one's clothes
        fascinating tales can be told

One morning when I stopped by to clean my duds
        in this room full of rows of rotating suds
        I heard more dirt than I needed to receive
        men talking about women they couldn't leave
        in fine Southern drawls they opened up and confessed
        gripes they just had to get off their chest

Their spouses gave them pleasure but twice as much pain
        can't live with 'em or without 'em one gentlemen complained
        he was folding shirts instead of playing poker
        his woman held the cards and took away the joker
        kept nagging him to earn more money dear
        trying to make him lose more weight and drink less beer
        he had to paint the den and the kitchen door
        and smoke his cigars out on the front porch

She nipped every day at his manly pride
        until he slipped away and found a young girl on the side
        bragging to his buddies in a cautionary tone
        this was only for their ears alone

When I had heard enough to want to change my mood
        I escaped to the other corner of the room
        where like in a sewing circle or coffee clutch
        some women were ragging just as much
        One gal's neighbor had found a man down the block
        and taken up a secret back door knock
        just don't ever tell her husband or he might get a gun
        if he ever found out what the two of them have done

After hearing these stories both tawdry and hot
        I couldn't help but connect the dots
        wouldn't it be funny and wouldn't it be strange
        if the couples mentioned were one and the same

MEETING OF THE RIVERS
(Paducah, KY)

High up on cemented steps watching the muddy Ohio's travel
          I gazed upstream and saw another river unravel
          joining forces making the water's path so wide
          it would take an athlete to swim to the other side

Tennessee and Kentucky rains descended to the flat plains
          as they passed downstream in a few bends
          these rivers will empty out again
          into the mighty Mississippi for a journey long and slow

Though content to watch these waters flow
          I wished I was a bird and could follow them as they go
          all the way down to the Gulf of Mexico

HILLBILLY CAFÉ
(Wickliffe, KY)

In the westernmost corner of the bluegrass state
          sits a small town café where breaded foods fill up one's plate
          pork chops in a large pan filled with bacon greases
          where mashed potatoes and sausage gravy rarely ceases

Home baked biscuits with margarine and jellies
          served to nearby farmers and local hillbillies
          even the blue jeaned gentleman painted on the mural outside
          has had more than his share of food that's been fried

TENNESSEE

CUMBERLAND RIVER BRIDGE
(Carthage, TN)

Pale turquoise girders rise up mightily over the still dark green waters below
    joining farm lands and farm hands from both sides
A hop, skip and jump and neighbors can howdy, talk crops and recipes
    without a risky swim or walkie-talkie
Tractors plow north and/or south with the same freedom as the cows graze

IF LOOKS COULD KILL
(Copperhill, TN)

As stark and desolate as toxic waste
    a living barely breathing example of caustic taste
A drive through this former company chemical venue
    makes one glad one is just passing through
I wouldn't wish a transfer here to friend or foe
    for if looks could kill there's a mean one here at Copperhill

TWO SIDES OF THE SMOKIES
(Gatlinburg, TN - Cherokee, NC)

Garish gleaming Gatlinburg garners its cash registers full blast
    motels signs register no vacancy and German chalets boast ski lifts
    miniature golf courses abound in this y'all spend family playground
Meanwhile in the low-key nation of Cherokee tourists are invited with camp, not hype
    as feathered natives in traditional drag
    flag the curious into the trading posts
Museums with stories of yesteryear's glories keep alive
    the remnants of a once proud tribe

CAMPING OUT IN A RENTED OLDS
(Nashville, TN)

No room at the inns in this Bible Belt city
    with no place to stay I felt like Joseph and Mary being turned away
How was I to know out-of-state pilgrims would fill every cranny
    every uncle, aunt, gramp and granny
    coming to pay their respects to the Grand Ol' Opry Fan Fair
30,000 extra tourists, country music purists have left me to stare at the real stars
    from the back of my rented Olds camping out in the hilly folds
    of Nashville's frilly outskirts tossing and turning to the steady thicket
    of crickets chirping in the stillness of the warm Southern night

TEXAS

DON'T MESS WITH TEXAS
(Whole State)

In this state highway signs not only have a message, they also carry an attitude
Any critter can litter from Maine to Nebraska and be an outlaw for a small price
But in the Lone Star if you throw stuff from your car this state will rake you
     even if the fee doesn't break you
You've messed with the big and the bad
    pardner, your hide is had

CITY CAFE
(Columbus, TX)

Not much passes in this time warp of a café, folks amble in slowly,
    two grampas at a back table smoke cigars
    while two grammas gab in front of a giant finned car
Pie slices in the display rack are as fresh as the counter and stools are old
    P,I,E,S stenciled in peeling letters painted gold
The waitress serves one-armed style holding her infant at her side
    as three generations stand time still
Here, living in the past keep bygone traditions from getting lost in a state so vast

SMOKESTACKS
(Beaumont, TX)

Today is so gray that as the refiner's vertical ringed cylinders
    spew out circular trails of spent exhaust
    one can hardly differentiate them from the clouds

THERE'S SOMETHING ELECTRIC IN THE AIR
(Dallas, TX)

As I stare into downtown Dallas' eyes
    from afar in my car speeding through one of her main arteries
    taking aim straight at her heartbeat
Fifty stories above her feet in neon towering over her broad skyscape
    an aura, a light shield surrounding
    her proud body eminates an architecture that isn't quite there
I swear, there's something eclectic
    there's something electric in the air

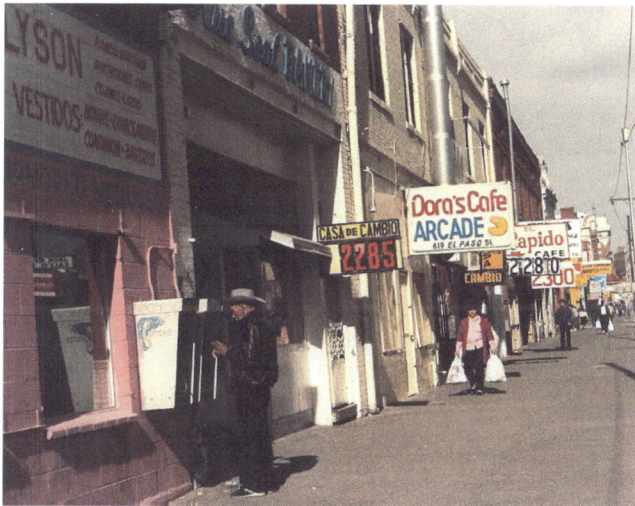

LITTLE MEXICO
(El Paso, TX)

Just a stone's throw from Mexico in a colorful barrio
    walkovers trek plastic bags filled with brand named goods

back to their neighborhoods across the border
Prices from ranch eggs to designer clothes fall dramatically
          as one goes forth each block north into la tierra de los gringos
In modern El Paso in the hills across town they no habla spanish
          wide southern drawls spread out in large Texan sprawls
While in Little Mexico los otros come and go daily
          like gypsies gaily in pursuit
          of as much of the American dream as they can carry home

WORKER BEES
(Houston, TX)

Darting between downtown Houston's giant glass towers
          a cascade of workers like a parade of bees
          file out with grateful post-five facial expressions
          combined with the exasperation that drones must feel
          after being couped upstairs in the corporate hive all day
Few notice the red-orange garb they wear
          as the fireball sun on the horizon bathes all in its delicate hues
Escapes preoccupy them as some race for the parking lots
          and their Mustangs and Porsches
          fighting the pesky sun out of their visors
While a dapper gent boards the bus to catch a window seat
          and a cowboy kicks up his heels with a do-si-do on Main Street

HIGHWAY 80 GRILL
(Longview, TX)

Hot lunches, fine food, the neon sign with rotating light bulbs flashed
> two couples sat at the counter gossiping until they got it right

The lone waitress was laughing her fool head off
> at some remarks that came out of the kitchen
> I sat on my stool trying to decide whether to laugh with them
> she brought my order of stuffed peppers as fast as McDonald's

Unexpected warmth followed from her mouth
> while serving cornbread, she bid me welcome to the South
> and cracked one of the corniest jokes I ever heard
> I laughed myself silly with every word

No entertainment charge was on the bill
> I was far from short-changed in Longview at the Highway 80 Grill

THERE AIN'T NO JUSTICE IN MARFA
(Marfa, TX)

There ain't no justice cries the statue erected in her honor
> she towers above the flat town garbed in classical gown
> disarmingly beaming her jurisprudence

For a century, though she's been polished and clean
> the hardware that once was hers alone is no more to be seen
> a disgruntled convict took aim with his shotgun to complain

True to his mark, he gave her scales a quick fall from grace
> something no one has made the effort to replace
> so be on your best behavior in any Marfan situation
> because justice in this town is still on vacation

LOW HILLS AND FLAT PLAINS
(Sanderson, TX)

Three hundred sixty degrees of low hills and flat plains, many miles of more of the same
    not a tree on the horizon, not a bird on the wing
      not a cloud in the sky, not a wisp of a breeze, just silence unrelenting
If it weren't for my Toyota breaking wind along the highway
    this West Texas terrain might pass unseen, unheard, and unnoticed

RIVERWALK
(San Antonio, TX)

Cutlery sounds resound across the water, waiters and diners converse in hushed tones
    lovers hold hands as they stroll, eyes transfixed by shafts of sunlight
    reflected from the river's surface
Travelers browse as echoes of conventioneers
    whooping it up in a Lone Star bar nearby filter through
Imported ices, sweets and spices lift one's spirit
    high above the Texas prairie from which the river rolls
Under a wisp of a breeze in an atmosphere warm and delicate
    is an oasis of graceful charm where Dixie shakes hands with the West
    in the shadow of the Alamo where San Antonio entertains her guests

LOUISIANA

DORSEY'S MOTEL
(Alexandria, LA)

On the other side of Alexandria's tracks on a street where soul is spoken
          where trickle down is a promise broken
In a neighborhood the city neglects these accommodations are circumspect
          just trailers and pit toilet situations
No triple A recommendations yet the poor folk who stay here have no reservations
          about ringing the bell at Dorsey's Motel

BATON ROUGE HARBOR
(Baton Rouge, LA)

The broad river's edges harbor no grudges
          as banks of oil money on the sandy wharf
          collect interest as well as mud
          in the shadow of government buildings
Architectural curiosities on bricks sit just above flood stage
          priests say mass in old cathedrals
          with a sprinkling of French for la belle age
Judge and jurists leave the bench and courtroom
          for a few minutes of reflection and find the river not guilty
Foghorns blast warnings as the blanket of evening
          tucks in the sleepy riverside streets and limits visibility
Commuters honk impatiently waiting for a drawbridge to open
          hoping for a quick span across the Mississippi River home

BAYOU MONOCHROME
(Catahoula Lake, LA)

The gray brown wintry cloud cover makes a monochrome
                  with the bare-trunked treetops and dried hanging moss
                  that call these sultry bayous home
Gray brown extends as far as the eye can see
                  even the birds who fly in flocked formation
                  camouflage perfectly with sky and trees
Still waters ripple only as stones fall or amphibians play a surface call
                  and that on this silent day is rare, if at all

WORKING MAN'S BUFFET
(Lafayette, LA)

All y'all can eat is the lunch blue plate special
                  for the hefty appetites of the local tradesman fellows

On vacation, it was time for my break
                  gumbo, sausage, red beans and rice
                  I simply could not forsake

So I put on a work shirt and sauntered inside
                  to join the noon crowd in line and ate 'til I was satisfied

In this Cajun capital where spicy food rules the day
                  not far from heaven at this working man's buffet

WE'LL MAKE IT THROUGH LUNCH
(Pineville, LA)

A gentle cool deep Southern winter morning
                sees Pineville's citizens' warming themselves at tables
                lined next to shelves of tiny pastries
                and a serve yourself coffee pot

The women and men sit separately
                conversations running genderly
                recipes followed and military posing
                cups measured and army bases closing
                time spent and civilian jobs lost
                family budgets at such a cost

How will we ever survive the crunch?
                oh well, we'll make it through lunch

OLD BUILDING ABANDONED
(Shreveport, LA)

A young black man dressed in brown tries to flag a ride down
                as he stands outside an old building abandoned
                four stories high with sixteen sets of planks over glass
                boarding each entry in patterns random

He sticks out his thumb in all directions to no avail
                while the warehouse covers up its poverty ashamed and frail
                both could use a lift

FLORIDA

LITTLE HAITI
(Belle Glade, FL)

Migrantly, vagrantly, they hang out on street corners
        biding time in front of the conch and stew beef parlors
The stark housing projects resonate with dark liasons
        while the main street puts on a friendlier face
Pawn shops and bargain stores
        earn what meager dollars can be found
Few are immune from poverty in this Caribbean transplant town

OUT OF THE SAME SOIL
(St Mark's, FL)

The corrugated tin roof is so rusty
        and the earthy colored shack beneath it so musty
        that they appear to be growing right out of the same soil
        as the rest of the inhabitants of this panhandle grove

FISH TAKING FLIGHT
(Jacksonville, FL)

Casting their hopes into the St. John's
      three young dark-skinned men pursue acrobatic mullet
      as the silvery fish skid over the flat water
      making concentric ripples on the river's surface

This juxtaposition of exquisite dimension
      fronts light beams from the other side
      shining down from the skyscrapers towering behind

Brown fishermen, silver prey, magenta clouds
      oncoming lights in the sultry Jacksonville twilight
      make a composition full enough
      to make the viewer as well as the fish take flight

SUGAR FIELDS
(Lake Okeechobee, FL)

Tall, sweet canes bend gracefully in the breeze from the everglades
their thin green blades form rows like cornfields in all directions
Irrigated canals with caressing trickling fingers
see to it that all is moist as if the tropical air
wasn't wet enough for these thirsty stalks

EVERGLADES CRANE
(Miles City, FL)

His beauty, bigness and overwhelming white coat
earn this crane more compliments than protection
as he stalks the swamps beside the everglades highway
If he could only store his jacket on a rack for special occasions
he wouldn't be subject of admiration and envy of friend and foe
wishing they could wear his fine feathered clothes

CALLE OCHO CAFE
(Miami, FL)

The electric blue counter winds around this Cuban cafe
like a slithery reptile making its daily foray
as bosomy waitresses search for hungry mouths to feed
The cook heats up his pots and pans filling custard cups with freshly made flan
scooping moros y cristianos serving media noche aficionados
Dark black beans and silky white rice steeped in savory spice
accompany many a diner's delight on this balmy Miami night

FAST LANE TRAILS
(Miami Beach, FL)

Turning the Bay of Biscayne into a sea of fleeting trails
        in his ever accelerating wake
The water skier barely outpaces the fast lane business deals
        closing in the high rises towering behind him

GEORGIA

CONFEDERATE GRAVES
(Atlanta, GA)

Rows and rows of plain white markers
       southern soldier's names like Jackson and Malone
       grave reminders of the volunteers for a once popular cause
Heroes both acknowledged and unknown fighting a valiant but losing battle
       where victory was defeated by a death rattle
A tragic reminder of brave fathers, sons, uncles and brothers
       whose blood was spilled for the freedom to deny freedom to others

EBENEZER BAPTIST CHURCH
(Atlanta, GA)

Black suits, white shirts, black ties
       black formal dresses with white borders
Sunday dressed black worshipers exit this famous sanctuary
       keeping the dream alive filling the morning with pride
Now that homage to history has been made
       it's time to get down to a "thank you Jesus" prayer breakfast

NORTH GEORGIA LUNCHEONETTE
(Carterville, GA)

Red-eyed gravy 'n biscuits, country ham 'n eggs
       good ol' boys are pinchin' at the waitresses legs
       black folk eat at the back of this behind the times cafe
Keep the skillet good 'n greasy, nothing changes day to day
Every thing has its purpose, every man has its place
Don't rock the boat, pass the cornbread,
       and, oh yes, don't forget to say grace

GAME ROOM
(Brunswick, GA)

Drinking, smoking, shooting, and gambling wait unashamed
       in this black sheep of Brunswick dive
       for neighborhood players who are game

RAILROAD CROSSING
(Valdosta, GA)

After waiting for what seemed like an eternity
       long enough for even small town clocks to start counting time
       the flatland freight finally finished pulling its hundred cars
       past the pickups and autos in line
With army surplus and feed mill customers
       patiently rapping their fingernails on their steering wheels
Valdosta's faithful heaved a collective sigh of relief
       as the caboose locomoted by
The red and white striped rail guard bellied up
       and life once again moved along its customary trail

SEA FOAM
(Tybee Island, GA)

Now you sea it, now you don't
        frothy foam builds its home on the wet Atlantic sandy banks
        only to surrender it to the sun or the next wave
        whichever gets there first

OKRA KING
(Waycross, GA)

Buckets and barrels of produce displayed
        fall pumpkins perched in autumnal parade
        under a twisted quonset tin roof's semi-shade
        from red ripe tomatoes to sweet melon's flesh
        salads of tomorrow beckon farm fresh
The living here is easy with what the red Georgia soil brings
        In a land of plenty that calls okra its king

NORTH CAROLINA

THE QUILTMAKER
(Chandler, NC)

Down the far end of a long gravel driveway
        where the sounds of passing tractors
        and pickups on the two-lane road hardly penetrate
The quiltmaker sews in her batten down cottage
        with a brook running at her back
        a garden of scraps at her feet
        and a homespun Quilts For Sale sign
        in front of her pioneer style cabin

JAMMING AT THE RUNNING BEAR
(Cherokee, NC)

The four-piece country band is perched on its tiny grandstand
        treating reservation locals to some party-minded vocals
        with a high-cheekboned lead singer
        putting his audience through the wringer
        mixing love ballads, uptempo rockers
        western oldies, and square dance cloggers
Folks get grooving before the night gets old
        and a wondrous sight to behold is two lard-filled ladies
        products of too many biscuits 'n gravies
        shaking hundreds of pounds of bouncing joy
        to the delight of the native girls and boys
        with guitar twanging to drums banging everywhere
        and the redskins jamming at the Running Bear

GOOD LISTENERS
(Woodrow, NC)

Two little 'uns take turns hangin' from the screen door
        as the front porch swing waits for a sitter
        under the faded red grocery sign
        which says its familiar howdy
The gossipy shopkeeper, mother of two and baseball fan
        will be glad to tell y'all about it
        fer as long as yer ears can stand it
Don't worry 'bout buyin' a thing
        good listeners are always welcome

NORTHEAST

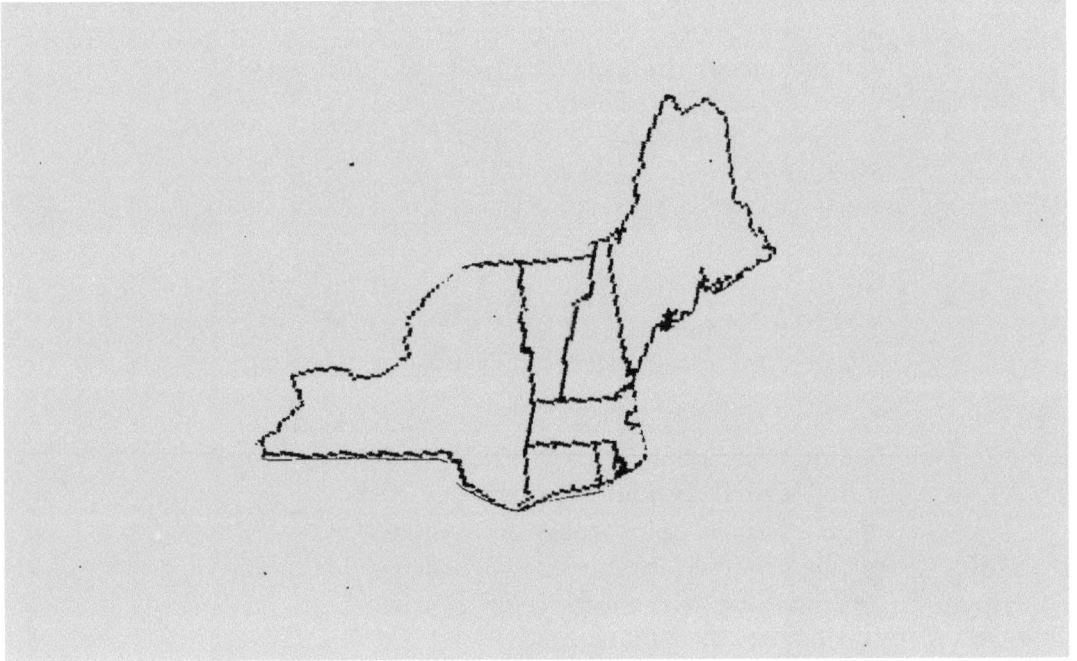

From the fashionable and not so chic urban edges of Manhattan to the quaint charms of rural upstate New York and New England to the rugged character of coastal Maine, the Northeast holds a wide variety of human and pastoral images. One is struck by the centuries-old architecture that fosters an atmosphere of convention and conformity in its stalwart citizens who cultivate the grit and self-reliance needed here to cope with the challenging environment.

NEW YORK

BROADWAY BUS DOWNTOWN
(New York City, NY)

On this busy thoroughfare nobody cares if I board the bus or not
　　　　　these passengers frozen in their isolated spots
　　　　　I deposit my token and see not a word dare be spoken
　　　　　or person looked straight in the eye
Is trust a word reserved for fool, if I drop my cool
　　　　　will out of town be written all over my face?
Why does my sunny California disposition seem so mispositioned?
　　　　　I refuse to shut the open lens of my perceptions
　　　　　but far from home, I'll "when in Rome"
　　　　　to this brazen bunch better left alone
I promise not to strike any conversation this time around
　　　　　as I ride the Broadway bus downtown

BULLY IN A BAKERY
(New York City, NY)

You talk too loud the bully shouted
　　　　　between the bagels and croissants next to our breakfast table
I tried to ignore his outburst
　　　　　because in Manhattan both talk and bullies are often in season

He retreated to the Kaiser rolls and we continued our conversation
　　　　　albeit a little more subdued as his eyes glazed like icing
　　　　　until he brandished a knife hanging at his waist
　　　　　not intended for slicing bread to taste

I felt like trumpeting your mother gives birth to mongrels
　　　　　but hushed for the moment as this dictator among Danish
　　　　　seeing his command temporarily obeyed
　　　　　like a barking dog retreated back to his lair

Not wishing to confront, nor to be held prisoner, I muttered softly
　　　　　while the ire of the other patrons like me grew
　　　　　until the baker, pastry knife in hand
　　　　　made a gesture that even bullies understand

The whimpering mutt who had been so pissy
　　　　　put his head beneath his legs, and acting like a sissy
　　　　　retired to the scum and dregs of his street poor existence

FASHION PRINCESS
(New York City, NY)

Standing in front of the plush leather jackets
       she makes a racket rattling off a list of demands
       to salesgirls waiting on her hand and foot
       Our Lady of the Fashion Statement in designer this and clothier that
From her Joan Crawford pumps to her zirconium veiled hat
       she shows Bloomingdales a grand display of
       attitude even royalty hardly gets away with
With loyalty to her plastic credit card scepter
       bowing only to the rich investor who's kept her
To the mirror she cries look at me, look at me
       who's the best dressed woman on this shopping spree

FROM HERE TO JOISY
(New York City, NY)

Am I a little too shrill for you the crazy lady shouts
       if you'd been through what I've been through
       then you'd be yelling this out

I was chasing my star on the Broadway scene
        when the lure of the streets grabbed me in my teens
        and I became a soft touch for heavy hands

Now I'm beggin' for crumbs in donut stands and sleeping in makeshift beds
        with only a shopping bag over my head
        wheeling around my dreams in a cart
        carrying the baggage of a lonely heart

Now mister don't tell me not to be so noisy I'll raise my voice from here to Joisy
        tell every bastard who ever let me down
        just how much I hate this town
Outa my way I'm spreading the news
        New York, New York has battered me blue

LESS FOR MORE
(New York City, NY)

I should have known when the menu said a la carte
        and its well-heeled patrons so young, hip and smart
        that this semi-French restaurant in Yuppie dress
        would promise more and deliver less all in the name of art
I couldn't pass up the chance to sample a plate of slender shreds
        of such tender yellows, greens and reds
        in a gallery they'd be heaven sent
        but to my appetite they hardly made a dent
My plate of duck drenched in wine, one piece in sauce so fine
        two gravies woven in ancient design
        I hated to disturb this chef d'oerve and its garni herb
        but hunger prevailed and it soon was inside of me
Delicious appetizer my gut replied
        now where's the main course it cried
        I looked to see if there was anything I had forsaken
        but the waiter said I'd already partaken it all
I prayed dessert would be the cure
        and when the pastry tray arrived with its array miniature
        I picked out a tidbit precious and sweet
        but hardly felt a thing when it I did eat
Now that the meal was complete
        the check nearly knocked me out of my seat
        I signed my VISA bill without pretext
        while my stomach cried where are we going next?

SKIING ON THE SUBWAY
(New York City, NY)

Holding on to stainless steel slings
        these urban skiers don't need poles to balance the bumps
        of the subway's stops, rattles and thumps
They merge with the car at every glitch
        as I cringe at every twitch
Like champion slalomers trained for competition
        they stay the course in hazardous condition
Brushing off every shock to the senses
        they make this cross-city trip look effortless
        while I work to keep my composure as well as my breakfast

POLKA PARTY
(Worcester, NY)

Outside the civic building with its old town charm
        a polka party was given for folks off the farm
With a potluck supper and home baked pies
        and accordion music for the German gals and guys
Getting in formation in their colorful clothes
        wearing petticoats and liederhose
Couples who've danced with each other for so many years
        circled round as spectators cheered
Just before the leaves started to fall a good time was had by all

VERMONT

DUNKIN' GOSSIP WITH THE DONUTS
(Barre, VT)

Down at Dunkin' Donuts they gossip all day
   among crullers and croissants with dismay
   discussing irresponsibilities
High-school dropouts and teen pregnancies
   of the welfare and the soon-to-be-on-it crowd
   in this once active New England mining town
A bit of Wyoming in Vermont, this blue-collar community
   has little immunity from its car passenger cruisers
   on late night avenues looking for trouble unforgiving
Ready to burst any chamber of commerce bubble of
   stable middle-class Yankee living

SIDEWALK CAFES
(Burlington, VT)

Shoppers walk up and down this warm friendly university town
   where every third store is a sidewalk café
   with chalkboard menus and tables lively and gay
Customers bring their dogs on leashes
   accompanying outdoor meals under warm breezes
   pooches obediently resting at their side
Waiters, diners, bowsers and browsers satisfied together
   sharing a pleasant evening in the Indian summer weather

DRAKES ON THE LAKE
(Lake Champlain, VT)

A flock of birds flies by in formation
        playing follow the leader to find a tranquil location
        descending one by one into the flat water below

Boats moored in Lake Champlain dry out after a passing light rain
        moisture gleams in the fading late afternoon sun
        before the harbor lights have begun to shine
        lighted trails across the lake in circling rippling lines

Passing boats send out their wakes
        as the ducks and drakes relax on the lake

NEW HAMPSHIRE

BELOW THE BELFRY
(Portsmouth, NH)

Its tall angular white steeple reaches skyward
       with an antique roman clock below the belfry
       and centuries old red bricks underneath
       surrounding rows of narrow stained glass windows
       make a fine portrait to bequeath to new generations
       a landmark surviving centuries in this central location
Modern day residents go about their business
       frequenting boutiques, bars, and eateries quite pleasant
       oblivious to the mystery of this history in their presence
While visitors and history buffs like me
       sit on wooden benches across the street
       to fantasize how life was led so long ago

DURGIN BRIDGE
(Sandwich, NH)

Dark brown wood weathered and old
        covers the bridge spanning the Cold River
        with only one lane for people and cars to cross

Pedestrians are welcome in this refuge
        especially if caught in a temporary deluge
        over 6-ton vehicles not advised at any cost
        or the bridge itself might be lost

Honk your horn before driving through
        especially if stormy weather occludes your view
        when crossing the rafters of this historic span
        that joins both sides of riparian land

PICKING BLUEBERRIES
(White Mountains, NH)

In the fading days of warm September air
        I stopped at a farm to pick my share
        of sweet globed fruit hanging from shrubs
        with printed instructions next to a small metal tubs

The honor system in place, just weigh before you leave
        do it yourself, we trust you won't deceive
        so I carried a bucket and rolled up my sleeves
        and filled it until I could pick no more

I was as honest as I could be
        though tasting every third berry to see
        that the crop maintained its fine quality this late in the season

When I checked out, I couldn't find any reason
        to weigh myself along with the harvest I had reaped
        but not to feel guilty for getting off cheap

I left a tip for the farm to cover any harm I may have done
        getting my fill on blueberry hill in the early autumn sun

MASSACHUSETTS

BEACON HILL
(Boston, MA)

Twists, turns, and cobblestones curve under trailing ferns
        lamp-lighted streets replete with mystery
        three-storied houses in quaint little rows
        of mansions and flats reeking with history
From terraced balconies up on high
        ivy and climbing vines hang down
        the sun streaks onto narrow pathways
        lined with leaves fallen on the ground

If these fenced walls could talk they'd reveal tales of generations
        pursuits of urban pleasures and treasures come and gone
        families joined, separated, and reunited
        personal and civic battles lost and won

Though there's been some change of names
        residences and situations somehow remain
        as new Hill dwellers replace the old
        similar dramas unwind and unfold
Meanwhile the Beacon winks and smiles
        shining a path down to Boston harbor that links for miles

FUNKY MUSIC AT COPLEY SQUARE
(Boston, MA)

Urban contemporary grooves play soulfully
        in the heart of the Boston
        funky music performed for free
Feel good rhythms with a sassy twist
        black and white musicians feeling it together
        sophisticated harmonies and jazzy riffs
        synthesized joys forever

Dancers gyrate across the lawns
        in spontaneous combustion, getting it on
Strangers clap to the beat and shake hands
        as the inner city rocks in motion with the band

Vibrations bounce from office buildings, stars shine bright
        celebrating sweet sounds of freedom
        as the liberty bell rings out in the summer night

MAINE

CONVERSION DIVERTED
(Biddeford, ME)

I had no idea I'd be getting into such a lurch
        when I stopped to take a photo of an old historic church
        in this small coastal Maine town where nostalgia enticed me
        an old woman saw me shooting and stopped to invite me
        to worship Christ as good Christians do there
        I said was Jewish and just passing through there

Though I thanked her politely and declined
        she wouldn't take my refusal and with a one-track mind
        accused me of heathenism and blasphemy
        turning my pastoral afternoon into tragic-comedy
        of absurd proportions sending my emotions into contortions

She raged out of control about saving my soul
        forcing me to yell that it was time to let me be
Then one of her friends walked by and diverted her soliloquy
        just long enough for me to walk away and set myself free

NATURE PRESERVE
(Kennebunkport, ME)

Wooden planked trails through leafy green forests and ferns
        every hundred feet or so they wind and turn
        into bridges crossing bogs and salt marshes
Frogs croak as birches form living arches
        not much wildlife is apparent at first
        but stay silent and you can hear birds and their shrilly outbursts
        guarding their homes where all and their kin are left alone
Don't stray off the path, off-road hikers forbidden
        from trampling the landscape in this refuge hidden
        a safety zone that protects and serves
        as a sanctuary at this lovely if not lively nature preserve

SHOREMAN'S CHOWDER
(Saco, ME)

In this shoreman's town I stopped for a meal
        at a dive of an eatery with a rough-hewn feel
The menu up on chalkboards and window signs of cardboard paper
        inside a motley crew of macho manual labor
        assembled seafood sandwiches as fast as they were able
        and brought bowls of white chowder to almost every table
No wine list here, only bottles of beer locals downed with a flurry
        then back to their jobs on the boats or nearby stores
        just a little chit-chat and not much more
For such a small price, large portions left me quite chipper
        at this industrial lunchroom known as The Skipper

HARBOR BOAT FISHERMAN
(York Harbor, ME)

As gray clouds above let loose their gentle precipitation
        he sits draped in his hooded rain gear situation
        holding his upright wooden spear in check
        perpendicular into the salt-covered deck
        as his fishing boat trolls out to sea
        in the flat gray waters around him

His shoulders hunched in anticipation
        will soon be needed as he pursues his daily catch
        of the slithering creatures swimming
        in the bay that surrounds him

He says a quick prayer to the ocean gods
        hoping today to improve his odds
        when he'll dip for bait in his tank to chuck it
        to attract hungry fish to fill his buckets
        and return home with enough to sell
        to the local customers who know him well
        for the freshly caught seafood meals he brings ashore

ABOUT THE AUTHOR

Cat Cohen was born in the 1940s near downtown LA and called the City Of Angels home for six decades before resettling in the high desert above Palm Springs. As a child he played along the walk of stars on Hollywood Boulevard and rubbed shoulders with the entertainment world early on, making two guest appearances on Art Linkletter's House Party TV show. At the age of ten his family moved to the Jewish neighborhood near Canter's Deli on Fairfax Avenue where he learned to fish pickles out of a barrel and haggle prices at local bakeries. His adolescence was spent in the San Fernando Valley before attending UCLA where he majored in music.

While enrolling in graduate school in classical composition, Cat also played in a rock band six nights a week in Redondo Beach. After a stint in the Peace Corps in Micronesia, he lived in Santa Monica a block from the ocean. Here he taught piano and wrote songs and musicals, several of which were recorded, produced, and performed. For many years he taught songwriting at UCLA Extension. During the 1980s he was involved in the political and social movements of LA's gay, HIV, and recovery communities, work he continues in the Coachella Valley today.

Cat is an author member of the **Palm Springs Writers Guild** with several self-published books on food, travel, music, and recovery. He is also a longtime **ASCAP** songwriter with pop, R&B, jazz and blues songs cut by recording artists **Cheryl Lynn**, **Syreeta**, **Freddie Hubbard**, and **Bo Diddley,** and has had his work featured in the **HBO** movie **The Rat Pack** and the **Universa**l feature film **Undercover Brother**. Currently, he performs as a pop music therapist and leads sing-alongs in hospitals, senior homes, and rehab centers.

www.catcohenauthor.com   www.catcohen.com
www.amazon.com/CatCohen/e/B00GG0QB74

[Photo by Joe Varga]

www.ingramcontent.com/pod-product-compliance
Lightning Source LLC
Chambersburg PA
CBHW042015080426
42735CB00002B/58